Rhino

The production of this book has
been generously supported by the
Simon Gibson Charitable Trust,
The Iliffe Family Charitable Trust,
the Manifold Trust and
the Rothschild Foundation.
Many many thanks to them all.

For Patrick

Animals in Art

Rhino

by Joanna Skipwith

Silver Jungle

Rhinoceroses

Many species on this planet are dying out. Some beautiful, graceful, strokable; some uncomfortably ugly. Of course it is the beautiful or extraordinary ones that we have grown to love through trips to the zoo, through films, books and small manageable toys that we are happy to keep in our bedrooms. The rhino does pretty well, it has character to make up for its lack of strokability, and it has captured the imagination of many artists for many centuries. It was used as a symbol by the Indus Valley traders four thousand years ago, and it is still used today as a logo by companies selling all sorts of things from jeeps and shoes to tea and crisps.

The car manufacturer and shoe company may have adopted rhinos because they look tough and purposeful, the tea

Left to right
White,
Black,
Indian,
Javan,
Sumatran.

company because they live in the countries where tea is grown, happily browsing on greenery. But crisps? Rhinos are not salty, crunchy or delicious. Perhaps they are used to sell crisps because their heads create such a wonderful and dynamic profile. They look cool and edgy, and you would never call a rhino, or a packet of crisps, 'Sissy'. Compared to the dinosaur, however, the rhino is not as popular as it should be. Whereas the dinosaurs died out millions of years ago, the rhino is still with us, *just*, trying very hard to mind its own business and keep a low profile.

This book includes images from several different countries. They are not necessarily the most famous, but each tells a story about a real rhinoceros or gives an idea of how the animal was regarded at that time. The text was written with a nine-year-old in mind, one that 'delights to abide in mud', but I hope that much of the information and many of the images will come as a surprise to the more 'mature' reader.

How this book was made
This book was printed in England on Revive Special Silk by Beacon Press using *pure*print environmental print technology. The paper, which combines recycled waste paper and new fibre from well-managed forests, is approved by the Forest Stewardship Council.

No oil painting

The rhinoceros. 'Prepoceros', as Ogden Nash once wrote. What an extraordinary animal with its massive barrel-like body, short yet nimble legs and large heavy head. And what an extraordinary name. It comes from the Greek *rhinos* meaning nose and *keras* meaning horn.

Although it is not a conventional beauty, it is magnificent, and its appearance has fascinated human beings for thousands of years. It has lived on this planet far longer than we have, perhaps 50 million years, and fossil forms have been found in North America and Europe. Now wild rhinos live only in parts of Africa and Asia. Their habitat ranges from the African savannas south of the Sahara to dense forests in tropical and subtropical regions.

Solitary creatures, rhinos are known to be rather grumpy. Males and females need their own space but they may, *just may*, share their feeding grounds and water holes with other animals. Even courtship can be an unfriendly affair, and males and females sometimes end up fighting.

Threatened by loss of habitat and killed for their horns, rhinos are among the most endangered species on Earth. In Asia the horns are ground up for use in traditional medicine. In Yemen they are made into handles for ornamental daggers called *jambiyas*.

Bushman engraving
Detail of a rock panel
Twyfelfontein, Namibia

This early image of a rhino is one of many carved on the sandstone boulders at Twyfelfontein in Namibia, an area of great spiritual and social importance for early African Bushmen. The ancient stones surround pools of water, which were visited by many generations of Bushmen, and there are hundreds of images of rhinos, giraffes, elephants and other animals etched into their flat surfaces. The Bushmen may have believed that the larger animals possessed supernatural powers, that the rhino, for example, could bring rain. Rock carvings are Africa's earliest works of art, dating back as far as 25,000 years. This one is at least 2,500 years old.

Five species

There are now only five species of rhino left. Four of these are critically endangered and survive in game reserves and national parks. There are two African species (the white and black rhino) and three Asian species – the Indian (or greater one-horned rhino), the Javan and the Sumatran. I find it difficult to remember how many horns they all have and what they get up to, so here are some notes.

The **white rhino** is the largest and heaviest. It has two horns and a wide mouth for grazing. It is the second-largest land mammal (the elephant is the largest), weighing up to 2,500 kg (5,500 lb), as heavy as a car. Though massive, it is probably the most docile and sociable, the one to invite to tea if you have to invite a rhino to tea.

The **black rhino** is lighter and faster (the sports model). It can reach a speed of 55 km/h (34 mph) at full charge and can accelerate or stop abruptly without losing its balance. It also has two horns and is the most aggressive. Steer well clear. Males of all five species fight, but the black rhino will fight to the death. Almost 50 per cent of males and 33 per cent of females die from wounds inflicted by their own species, the *worst* statistics among mammals.

Andy Warhol
American, 1928–87
Black Rhinoceros, for *Endangered Species*
Screenprint published in 1983 by Ronald Feldman Fine Arts Inc., New York

In 1983 Andy Warhol was commissioned by Ronald Feldman Fine Arts to create a series of prints on endangered animals. The black rhino, African elephant and orang-utan were among the 10 animals chosen to be given star treatment in Warhol's 'Factory', as he called his studio. By then he was world famous and had produced series upon series of brightly coloured screenprints of well-known faces, including Marilyn Monroe, Elvis Presley and Chairman Mao. He was a leading figure in the Pop Art movement, choosing to use everyday mass-produced images, whether Coca-Cola bottles, Campbell's soup cans or press photographs of film stars.

Asian rhinos

The **Indian** rhino has great folds of loose skin and looks as if it is wearing a suit of armour. It has one horn and is also pretty bad tempered. It is the one that has inspired most of the artists in this book. Not only is it the most surprising and interesting mixture of pattern and shape, it is also the species that was captured and shipped to Europe most often.

The **Javan** is the shyest and the most rare. It is so shy and secretive that hardly anyone has managed to find it. There may be a few hiding in the tropical forests of western Java, well away from poachers and conservationists, but there are roughly 65 known to be alive, in two reserves, one in Java, one in Vietnam. The Javan rhino has one horn and is most like the Indian rhino in appearance, but smaller. Invite it to tea, by all means, but it won't come.

The **Sumatran** is the hairy one. Yes, hairy. It is the least evolved and closest to the prehistoric woolly rhinoceros. It has two horns, is also shy and solitary and is the smallest of the five species. When young, it has a thick coat of reddish-brown hair, which thins and becomes more bristly as the animal grows, though the ears often remain furry. There may be as few as 300 left, living in small populations in Indonesia and Malaysia.

Vehicle of the gods
Khmer stone frieze
Cambodia, 12th century

This rare frieze carved from stone is thought to represent the Hindu god Indra riding on a rhinoceros. Indra was usually shown riding an elephant or a horse. He was rather like Jupiter, a Hindu version, sexy and aggressive, in charge of thunderbolts and lightning, and able to transform himself into any shape and any creature. The frieze is similar in style to those found at the famous Khmer temple of Angkor Wat where Agni, the god of fire, is shown riding a rhinoceros, as is the demon Bana. The small dainty rhino with smooth though patterned skin is probably a Javan rhino.

Indus Valley seals

The earliest images of the Indian rhino appear in small seals that survive from the Indus Valley civilisation and date from about 2,600 BC. In the 1920s archaeologists discovered a network of lost cities stretching across India, Pakistan and Afghanistan. The capital cities were Harappa in the Indian Punjab and Mohenjo-daro on the west bank of the Indus River in Pakistan. The seals, made from soft soapstone, were carved, polished and fired in a kiln to harden. They could then be stamped into soft materials such as clay and the image transferred.

Most of the simple designs are of animals, and the unicorn is the most common motif. The reverse side of the seals often has a boss with a hole, like a loop on an old-fashioned button. It is thought that thick cord was threaded through the hole when bundles of goods were being wrapped up. The seals would act like tags or labels to identify the trader, in the same way that the World Wildlife Fund now uses the panda on their merchandise. The inscriptions have not been deciphered yet. If it can be proved that they represent text rather than symbols, then these tiny square seals could provide the earliest known alphabet.

Four Indus Valley seals dating from 2,600–1900 BC

A
Carved impression of a rhinoceros
Fired steatite
National Museum of Pakistan, Karachi

B
Raised impression of a rhinoceros
Mohenjo-daro Museum, Pakistan

C
Pasupati seal
Fired steatite
National Museum of India, New Delhi

D
Carved impression of a unicorn
Fired steatite
Harappa Museum, Pakistan

A

B

C

D

Dürer's rhino

Albrecht Dürer became the most famous German artist of his time through the distribution of his prints. His rhinoceros became famous too, a 'blueprint' that was copied for many decades. Captured in India, it was shipped to Portugal in 1515 as part of an exotic cargo (together with peppers, cinnamon, rhubarb, incense and cloves). It was a gift for the Portuguese king Dom Manuel I and was the first rhinoceros to arrive in Europe alive since the 3rd century.

Seven months later, having refused to take part in a fight with one of the king's elephants, the peace-loving rhino was dressed up in a velvet collar, garlanded with flowers and sent off on another boat to Italy as a gift to Pope Leo X. It was reported to have stopped off in Marseilles, where the French king staged a mock battle and launched oranges at it (pretend cannonballs). This long-suffering present never reached Rome. The ship sank off the Italian coast, and the chained rhinoceros sank with it. How surprised it would be to know that it is now the most famous rhinoceros in the history of art.

It is thought that Dürer copied the image from a sketch sent out with a newsletter and, as you can see, he got rather carried away. He had designed armour in Nuremberg, and it seems that he could not resist designing some for the rhinoceros as well.

Albrecht Dürer
German, 1471–1528
The Rhinoceros, 1515
Engraving given to Maximilian I by the King of Lisbon. Private Collection

Dürer was born in Nuremberg where craftsmanship thrived. His father was a goldsmith and he learnt from him how to draw and engrave at a young age. He later learnt to design woodcuts and worked as an apprentice in Basel, a city then famous for its book production. This print had such an impact on other artists that fanciful rhinos, with extra horns, kept multiplying, appearing in ceramics, tapestries and paintings across Europe. You will find several in this book. It is perhaps thanks to Dürer that the rhinoceros had the reputation of being bullet-proof and why the Germans call the Indian rhinoceros *Panzernashorn* (the tank rhinoceros).

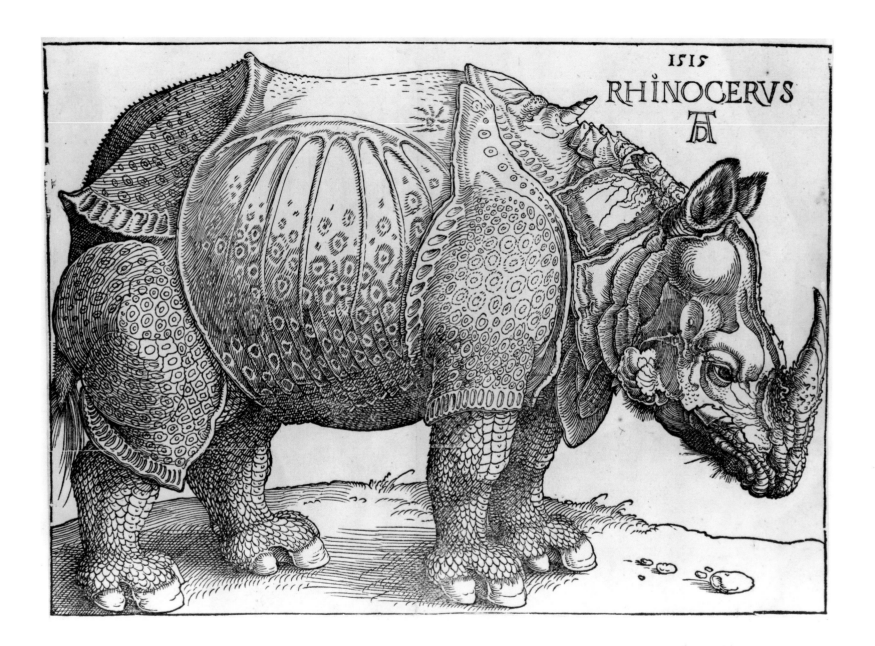

Toes to nose

Did you know that the rhinoceros is a perissodactyl. A what? Why, an odd-toed ungulate, of course. An odd-toed ungulate? Yes. It is a mammal with hooves and odd-numbered toes, like the horse (which used to have three toes many millions of years ago, but now has only one). The rhinoceros, with its three toes, is in fact more closely related to the horse than it is to the hippopotamus, which has an even number of four toes. The tracks of a Sumatran rhino look like the ace of clubs.

Rhinos have particularly poor eyesight and would probably not notice you if you stood still at a distance of 30 metres (100 ft). Their hearing is very good, however, and they can pick up even quiet sounds with their swivelling tubular ears. They rely most of all on their sense of smell, using their nose to find food and to track down a mate. Unlike us, their nostrils are bigger than their eyes. So ... if you come across a stray rhino, keep very still, keep very quiet and whatever you do, try not to smell like another rhinoceros.

Zoo rhinos tend to be very quiet, but in the wild rhinos can be quite noisy. Apparently they can snort, moo, puff, roar, squeal, shriek and honk.

Jean-Gabriel Prêtre
French, 1780–1845
Javan Rhinoceros, c. 1830–40
Watercolour on paper

Jean-Gabriel Prêtre was a well-known *animalier*, the French name for a natural history painter. He was employed by the natural history museum in Paris and by Empress Josephine to record the animals in their collections. Before the invention of photography, skilful illustration was the only method of recording the different species and sharing knowledge about them through prints in books. This Javan rhino with its smooth outline would have been difficult to print as each colour had to be printed separately, fitting *exactly* over the previous outline to avoid fuzzy edges. It wouldn't have mattered so much with the hairy Sumatran rhino.

That nose!

The Indian and Javan rhinos have a single horn. Black and white rhinos (the two African species) and the Sumatran rhino all have two horns, with the front one usually larger. Unlike the horns of cattle and antelope, rhino horns do not grow from the skull and are not made of bone. They grow from the skin and are made of keratin fibres – the same material as our hair and fingernails.

Although white rhinos will rub noses and horns with each other as a gesture of friendship, most rhinos use their horns as weapons – the females to protect their calves from predators, the males to attack each other.

The rhino's horn has been its downfall. In demand for centuries, often mistaken for the fabled unicorn horn, it is still believed by some to have magical powers. In the Middle Ages, Arab traders made handsome profits selling rhino horn to Europeans as unicorn horn. Even Queen Elizabeth I was hoodwinked. A 'unicorn horn' was one of her most treasured possessions and she kept it in her bedroom at Windsor Castle. Unicorn horn was an officially recognised drug in England until 1741.

Giovanni Battista della Porta
Italian, 1535–1615
Naso molto grande (Very large nose)
Woodcut from *Della Fisionomia dell'Huomo*, 1603. First published in Latin in 1586 as *De humana physiognomia*

Giovanni Battista della Porta began studying Latin at the age of six and spent much of his childhood in libraries studying chemistry, botany, alchemy, medicine, astrology and witchcraft. This image of the two noses is one of many illustrations in his book *Della Fisionomia dell'Huomo*, in which he attempts to show that you can tell a man's character from his physical appearance. Della Porta thought, for example, that if you looked like a donkey, you were likely to be timid and stupid. If you looked like a lion, you might be courageous. And if you had a large nose, you might be rather 'sniffy' about other people's ideas. Angelo Politiano, the owner of this particular nose, was a learned professor. Perhaps he made the mistake of dismissing one of Della Porta's theories ...

That skin!

Not only is the rhinoceros busy being a perissodactyl, or an odd-toed ungulate, or just a plain old short-sighted moody rhinoceros, it is also busy being a pachyderm, which means that it has very thick skin. Thick skin that gets hot and uncomfortable and needs to cool down, preferably in a mud bath. In Africa, when the mud holes dry out and wallowing is not possible, rhinos take dust baths instead.

The black rhino is not black and the white rhino is not white. All five species of rhinoceros are grey, and like elephants they take on the colour of the soil where they live because they love to roll in the dust or mud.

A good coating of mud helps to protect the rhino's skin from flies and ticks, for although the skin is thick, the blood vessels lie just below a thin outer layer. African rhinos are lucky to attract friendly birds called ox-peckers, which not only eat the ticks they find on the rhino's skin, but also act as an alarm system, flying off as soon as they sense danger. Their name in Swahili is *askari wa kifaru*, which means 'the rhino's guard'.

Eric Carle
American, b. 1929
The Rhinoceros, originally published in *Animals, Animals*, illustrated by Eric Carle, compiled by Laura Whipple
Copyright ©1989. All rights reserved

Eric Carle worked as a graphic designer and as an art director for an advertising agency before illustrating his first children's book *Brown Bear, Brown Bear, What Do You See?* It is still a favourite, but *The Very Hungry Caterpillar*, which he both wrote and illustrated, is his most popular. Published in 1969, it is still munching its way across the globe and has been translated into more than 30 different languages. Eric Carle creates his cheerful and striking collage illustrations using hand-painted tissue papers, which he cuts or tears to create an image or character.

Just so

According to Rudyard Kipling, who wrote the *Just So Stories*, there is a good reason why the rhinoceros has great folds of skin and a bad temper. It is because its skin is full of cake crumbs and currants, which tickle it like mad. Perhaps you already know 'How the Rhinoceros got his Skin', if not here is a short summary.

One day, on the shores of the Red Sea, a very bad-mannered rhinoceros called Strorks ate a delicious fruit cake freshly baked by Mr Pestonjee Bomonjee. The rhinoceros spiked the cake with its horn, gobbled it down without so much as a please or thank you, and sauntered off. Pestonjee Bomonjee was most upset ... but he did get his own back one hot day when Strorks decided to go for a swim.

In those days, according to Kipling, the rhinoceros skin was removable. It fitted very snugly and buttoned up underneath its belly, rather like a coat. When Strorks slipped it off and left it on the beach, Bomonjee filled it with handfuls of cake crumbs and burnt currants. Poor old Strorks, it didn't feel quite right when he put it back on again. He rolled and rolled on the sand, he rubbed and rubbed against a palm tree, but it made no difference. The cake crumbs were inside his skin and Oh how they tickled.

Joseph Rudyard Kipling
British 1865–1936
How the Rhinoceros got his Skin
Illustrations to the *Just So Stories*, 1902
First published as a book by Macmillan in 1902. British Library, London

Rudyard Kipling drew this rhinoceros himself and all the illustrations for the first edition of the *Just So Stories*. Full of comical names and enchanting nonsense, it is one of his most popular books for children. Kipling was born in Bombay (now Mumbai) in India, and his father taught at the local art school. Sent back to England at the age of five, he had a miserable time at boarding school and with foster parents, but returned to India in 1882 and worked there as a journalist for eight years. Later, in 1898, he began to visit Africa and to collect together more answers for those tricky questions: How *did* the rhinoceros get his skin? How *did* the camel get his hump?

Giant lawnmowers

The rhinoceros takes its responsibilities very seriously. Not only is it busy being a perissodactyl, an odd-toed ungulate and a pachyderm, it is also busy being a megaherbivore. In fact, being a megaherbivore is almost a full-time job and involves eating an enormous amount of greenery. The larger you are the more you have to eat. White rhinos, which can grow up to 1.8 metres (6 ft) tall and weigh up to 2,500 kg (5,500 lb) have wide, square-shaped mouths, ideally suited to graze on grass. Black rhinos prefer the foliage of trees and bushes. Their flexible upper lip is triangular and similar to the tip of an elephant trunk. It helps them to choose the leaves they want and tug them towards their mouths. The Javan and Sumatran rhinos mow their way through the sub-tropical forests, often pushing over young trees to reach the new shoots and leaves. They also eat bamboo and fruits.

Rhinos love water and need plenty of it for drinking and wallowing. In captivity white rhinos will drink up to 80 litres a day, but in the wild they may have to go without for 2–4 days. In the dry season, they will dig for water in dried river beds. Indian rhinos spend many happy hours wading deep into the lakes and flood plains to browse on grasses and water lilies. And Sumatran rhinos are surprisingly good swimmers.

Deccan School, India
An Indian miniature of a rhinoceros, c. 1750 Gouache, after an engraving by Dr James Parsons

This rhinoceros travelled from India by boat to London in 1739. It was the second rhinoceros to arrive in London, and was displayed in Red Lion Square and in Eagle Street, where you could go along and see it for two shillings and sixpence. It probably did not last very long. It was sketched, however, by Dr James Parsons, an early 'rhinocerologist'. The sketches were made into engravings and published in the *Philosophical Transactions of the Royal Society*, a scientific journal that would have been circulated across Europe. One journal managed to find its way back to India and the illustration of the rhino was copied by an Indian artist.

For weddings

Who is Katharina Payrsberg and what is she doing perched on a rhinoceros on her wedding day, in Innsbruck on 15 February 1580? I have no idea. Apparently she was a rich heiress who married the well-connected Johann Lipsteinsky von Kolwrat, a courtier of Archduke Ferdinand II. Sadly, it is very unlikely that Katharina chose this particular form of transport. In 1580 only one rhinoceros is known to have been alive in Europe, and it was living with Philip II of Spain in his palace outside Madrid. It is more likely that the archduke, who planned the festivities, got carried away with the pageants, arranging for his horses to be disguised as more exotic beasts, using papier-mâché. It is also possible that he was a little overexcited when instructing his court painter to make a record of the day's events.

If not Katharina, has anyone ridden a rhinoceros? There are references to warriors riding rhinos in early Persian manuscripts. In the *Dastan of Amir Hamzah*, a certain Gustahm bin Ashk rides into town on one, and a manuscript of the *Shah-Nama* shows the hero Jahangir, on horseback, battling against the 'Evil Champion Hizabr' on a rhinoceros. There are stories of knights in the Khmer army riding into battle on rhinos, but perhaps the writers and artists were trying to emphasise the bravery of their heroes or the brute force of the enemy.

The Marriage Procession of Katharina Payrsberg. A page from a book of festivities engraved by Sigmund Elsässer on 36 parchment leaves, Innsbruck, 1580 Schloss Ambras, Innsbruck

Festival books were supposed to record important events in European courts: weddings, baptisms and coronations. Festivities were recorded in prose or verse that often drifted off into the realms of fantasy, and those that commissioned the records were often portrayed as gods. In this book Archduke Ferdinand II is shown as Jupiter, in a carriage drawn by three eagles. Katharina is Cybele, the goddess of nature and fertility, who could tame wild animals. The artists and writers were encouraged to use their skills to create an image of their employers as powerful, virtuous and cultured.

And a funeral

Although the elephant has been harnessed and put to work, would the smaller and more unpredictable rhino have been worth the effort? Probably not. Though incredibly strong, they are a liability. When the Mombasa–Nairobi railway was built in Africa at the beginning of the 20th century, the black rhinos were most disapproving. They regularly charged at the steam trains, often derailing engines and coaches. And attempts to move rhinos from one enclosure to another at London Zoo in the 1860s always seem to have involved at least 24 men, several ropes and a certain amount of cursing.

In this tapestry panel, the rhinos are part of an important funeral procession, the funeral of Mausolus, independent ruler of Caria (south-western Turkey) from 377–353 BC. After his death, his distraught queen and sister, Artemisia, built an impressive funeral monument for him, designed and decorated by the best Greek architects and sculptors of the time. It was one of the seven wonders of the world, sadly destroyed by a series of earthquakes.

According to the Greek poet Homer, and later Herodotus, the Carians were military experts, who hired themselves out in turn to the Trojans, Persians, Egyptians and Greeks. Perhaps if anyone can discipline a rhino, a Carian can.

The rhinoceros chariot
from *The Story of Artemisia*
Tapestry panel, *c*. 1610
From a cartoon by Antoine Caron and Henri Lerambert
Mobilier National, Paris

Queen Artemisia is said to have missed her husband so much that she not only built his famous mausoleum at Halicarnassus but also drank his ashes mixed with water. Though pining away (she died two years after him and was also buried in the mausoleum), she successfully fought off an invasion from nearby Rhodes. She had inherited warrior blood and was descended from Queen Artemisia I, an ally of the Persian king Xerxes, who fought against the Greeks.

Clara

Clara was *the* A-list celebrity rhino. She toured Europe for 17 years from 1741–58 with her Dutch owner Douwemout van der Meer, travelling to Holland, Germany, Switzerland, France, Italy, Austria, Poland and Britain. People flocked to see her. She was admired by Frederick the Great in Berlin, by Empress Maria Theresa in Vienna, by Augustus III in Dresden and by Louis XV at Versailles. And the royals came to her, visiting her in fish markets, town squares, inns and orangeries. She was sketched by artists, goldsmiths, clockmakers, toymakers, porcelain decorators and printmakers. She inspired poetry and influenced Paris fashion, sparking off 'rhinomania'. Even two famous philosophers, Voltaire and Maupertuis, quarrelled over her.

Clara, as she was nicknamed in Germany, had been captured as a young calf in Assam in India. She was given to the director of the Dutch East India Company and treated by him as a pet, allowed to run around indoors and eat from a plate. At some point this arrangement must have become impractical and she was sold to Van der Meer who perhaps saw her as a chance to change career, from sea captain to showman. He shipped her back home to Rotterdam, first stop of their famous European tour. Van der Meer proved to be a brilliant publicist, producing posters in advance of their arrival at each city and souvenirs to buy: prints and medals in copper or silver.

Johann Elias Ridinger
German, 1698–1767
Rhinoceros Resting on its Side, 1748
Graphite on paper
Courtauld Institute of Art Gallery, London

Ridinger was a popular engraver who produced many prints of animals, often hunting scenes. He made six drawings of Clara on 12 June 1748 during her visit to Augsburg in Germany. By October she was in Wurzburg, where she was very popular and was given the name *Jungfer Clara* (Miss Clara). Though there are several paintings and engravings of Clara, this informal sketch of her resting is my favourite.

Oops!

It can happen to any celebrity on tour. Something can let you down: your voice, your nose, your manager or your brother. It happened to Clara, in Rome in 1750. Her nose, or rather her horn, fell off. Rhinos in the wild rarely shed their horns, but it does happen in captivity. Clara had been rubbing her horn against her enclosure, sometimes a sign of boredom or anxiety, but this was not necessarily the cause. Perhaps her unusual diet, which included a fair amount of beer and bread, was partly to blame.

Van der Meer must have grown very fond of his valuable travelling companion and would have looked after her as well as he could given the limited knowledge and availability of her ideal diet. He escorted her in great style, and she travelled in a specially designed wagon with her support team in tow. To make up for the lack of mud baths, he rubbed her with fish oil (then considered the best moisturiser for rhinos), and Clara is recorded as having been very affectionate towards him. Unfortunately, however, her frequent stays at inns did not help her drinking habit. She had developed a taste for beer and wine at an early age, much to the delight of the sailors who brought her over from Calcutta.

Horn or no horn, the Venetians were thrilled to see her when she arrived in Venice at Carnival time in 1751.

Pietro Longhi
Italian, 1702–85
The Rhinoceros, 1751
Oil on canvas
Ca' Rezzonico, Museo del Settecento, Venice

Longhi recorded everyday life in Venice, and his paintings provide much information about the customs and costume of the city in the 18th century. Carnival time in Venice still attracts thousands of tourists. At the time of this painting, it was an obvious destination for anyone making money from an unusual exhibit, whether a rhino or a giant. The painting was commissioned by a Venetian nobleman Giovanni Grimarni dei Servi (a later version is in the National Gallery in London). The man holding a whip and Clara's missing horn is probably her keeper. The young man on the right with a long pipe may be her owner, Douwemout van der Meer.

Special footnote for rhinocerologists and art historians: this could be the earliest painting of rhino poo.

Caramba!

Le cheval rayé (The zebra)
in the set of *Les Nouvelles Indes, c.* 1775
Detail from a tapestry woven at the
Gobelins factory, after a cartoon by
François Desportes
Kunsthistorisches Museum, Vienna

Tapestries gave warmth and colour to the
bare stone walls of Europe's castles and
palaces. They depicted historical events,
legends, allegories and often landscapes
that brought together exotic animals
from different foreign countries. The
Gobelins factory in Paris made the finest
tapestries in Europe, and made them
exclusively for the French king Louis XIV
during the 17th century.

Animals of different shapes and sizes,
sometimes the wrong shapes and sizes,
were crowded in amongst exotic foliage,
picked from pattern books or transferred
from 'cartoons' rather than drawn from
life. This tapestry is part of a set
representing South America, not known
to be teeming with Indian rhinos or
African zebras.

Clara had already visited Paris and
Versailles by the time this tapestry
was woven and had cleared up many
misunderstandings about what a
rhinoceros actually looked like. The
cartoon for this tapestry had been drawn
up in 1737, however, and was based on
earlier tapestries woven in 1687.

Miss Bet

How many men does it take to pull a rhino out of a frozen pond? 16?
No, 26, as demonstrated by Miss Bet at London Zoo in 1870. It had
snowed during the night on 27 December, covering the ground with
a thick white blanket and freezing over the pool in Miss Bet's enclosure.
Miss Bet, an Indian rhinoceros, had never seen snow before. When
turned out of her 'den' that morning, she could not distinguish the
ground from the pool, she promptly walked on to the ice and, CRASH,
disappeared underneath it.

The keepers ran to find Mr Abraham Dee Bartlett, the quick-thinking
Superintendent, the only man to be trusted in a crisis. He knocked out
the plug, summoned all available keepers and set to work pouring
barrow-loads of gravel into the icy water to give Miss Bet a foothold.
A rope was then passed around her bottom and 26 keepers managed
to haul her out after much heaving (the artist has shown only 16).
Mr Bartlett had left the sliding gate of the enclosure open, just wide
enough to let out one man at a time, but not the rhino. The keepers
rushed to the gate, but the first man, 'naturally stout, and possibly
stouter at Christmas time than usual' was too fat to squeeze through.
He became stuck, leaving his 25 colleagues trapped. Fortunately,
Miss Bet was a little out of breath and more interested in her breakfast
that morning.

Ernest Griset
French, 1844–1907
Miss Bet, 1871
Watercolour on paper
The Zoological Society of London

Born in France, Griset came to England
as a child and lived close to London Zoo,
where he often drew the animals. He
illustrated many books and magazines at
a time when Charles Darwin's theory of
evolution was creating much excitement
and many opportunities for artists who
could combine accuracy and humour.
When *The Times* mistakenly announced
his death, they described him as 'an
admirable and apparently inexhaustible
draughtsman who possessed much
satirical power and produced countless
drawings in grotesque of animals and
human savages, which wise collectors
obtained for trivial sums at an untidy little
shop near Leicester Square.' A week later,
the newspaper admitted that he was alive
and well. I am not sure that they ever
apologised to the Africans or the shop.

Rhino versus elephant

It was Pliny the Elder (AD 23–79), a Roman soldier and scholar, who spread the rumour that the rhino and elephant were bitter enemies. In his 37-volume *Natural History*, he wrote that the rhinoceros would *always* attack an elephant whenever it came across one, first sharpening its horn on a rock, then charging head down and goring the elephant, ripping into its soft underbelly. Pliny's words, translated from Latin into German, were reproduced on Dürer's print, and Van der Meer used them on posters to drum up interest in Clara.

When Dom Manuel I of Portugal, the proud owner of both Dürer's rhino and an elephant, decided to put this theory to the test in 1515, he was most disappointed when the rhino ignored the elephant and the elephant scarpered off through the streets of Lisbon.

In India in the 16th and 17th centuries, elephants were trained for battle and for hunting expeditions. They were encouraged to attack each other, goaded on by riders and spectators, but separated by a low wall so that they did not kill each other. It was a popular form of entertainment for the Rajput princes, and sometimes a rhino would be pitched against an elephant. Though the elephant is stronger, it is very vulnerable if the rhino can get underneath it.

Jan van Kessel the elder
Flemish, 1626–79
Detail from a collection of panels representing Africa from the cycle *The Four Continents*, 1664–6
Oil on copper, Alte Pinakothek, Munich

Jan van Kessel was born in Antwerp. His father was a painter and his mother a Brueghel, the daughter of Jan 'Velvet' Brueghel. He is best known for his paintings of flowers and insects, often on small copper panels, which were used to decorate cabinets. At that time there was a growing interest in natural history and in creating personal collections of insects and dried flowers. This panel is one of a group representing Africa. Apart from Dürer's Indian rhinoceros, other 'African' animals include tigers, walruses, even mermaids swimming off the coast of Madagascar. Van Kessel seems to have enjoyed painting butterflies, caterpillars and beetles most of all, and sometimes signed his name as a collection of tiny caterpillars.

Round two

It is not surprising if there was bad feeling between the two pachyderms when pitched against each other by bloodthirsty Romans or Indian princes, but there are occasions when they fight in the wild without too much prompting. They don't like waiting in the queue when water is scarce. Male elephants, in particular, can be lethal when in the grip of 'musth', a substance secreted from glands in their temples. But elephants and rhinos of all species can live happily alongside each other. Some are even friendly enough to pull each other's tails as a joke.

As with most species, female rhinos can be particularly aggressive when defending their young. They have only one calf at a time and form a strong bond with it. The calf is usually weaned after two years but will stay with its mother until she is ready to give birth again, two to four years later. Nursing mothers are very protective, and black rhinos have been known to kill lions to defend a calf. The fathers leave the females a few days after mating and play no part in the upbringing of their children.

Laurent de Brunhoff
French, b. 1925
Illustration from *Babar's Little Girl Makes a Friend*, first published in 1990.

Laurent de Brunhoff is the son of Jean de Brunhoff who drew the first images of Babar the elephant in his smart green suit. His father died in 1937, but since 1946 Laurent de Brunhoff has created and illustrated his own adventures for this much-loved character. In this story, Babar's young daughter Isabelle becomes friendly with Vic, the son of King Rataxes ... a rhinoceros! The parents of both children are most disapproving; there has been a longstanding family feud. Romeo and Juliet? Something along those lines. Here, King Rataxes and Lady Rataxes confront Babar and Celeste. The elephants are quite reasonable; the rhinos do most of the shouting.

We love you to bits

Rhinos are threatened by loss of habitat and by the constant demand for their horn. It is our species (*Homo sapiens*, meaning wise man) that is responsible. Large swathes of Africa and Malaysia were cleared during the last century for the rubber trade. Chunks of India were cleared to grow tea. Southern Asia is now under similar pressure from deforestation, particularly with the rise in demand for palm oil.

All five species are still poached for their horn despite international efforts to prevent this trade. In Asia the horns are ground up for use in traditional medicine, and are thought to cure anything from fever to food poisoning. In Yemen, daggers with rhino horn handles are a symbol of strength and bravery, and rhino horn is bought illegally on the black market. The current rate is $1,200 per kilo, so a black rhino carries about $3,600 worth of horn. It surely looks better on the end of its nose than it does anywhere else, even if studded with silver and slung from the waist of a handsome warrior.

Ceratotherium simum, Diceros bicornis, Rhinoceros unicornis, Rhinoceros sondaicus, Dicerorhinus sumatrensis. These are the names we have chosen to classify the five species. If the rhino had to classify ours, I think it might choose a different name from *Homo sapiens*, something rather rude.

Salvador Dalí
Spanish, 1904–89
Rhinocerotic Disintegration of the Illissus of Phidias, 1954
Oil on canvas, Gala-Salvador Dalí Foundation, Figueres, Spain

Dalí's paintings combine the details of observed reality with the details of his imagination. He was an important member of a group of artists and poets called the Surrealists, though they later expelled him. Recognised by them as a creative genius, there were nevertheless mutterings that he was 'a real menace', 'a mad man' and 'obsessed with sex'. He certainly became obsessed with rhinos and their horns, which although a symbol of sexual and mystical power, he also considered to be a perfect logarithmic spiral. You will find lots of horns in this painting and at least four rhino heads. Imagine that the rock in the sea is a horn if you need a starting point.

Never say die

Some say that 'the perissodactyls are an outmoded group' (*harrumph*) and that 'humanity cannot prevent the eventual extinction of the rhinoceros'. Well, we can at least try, and several organisations, including Save the Rhino International, try very hard.

The African species have received more attention in recent years and efforts to protect them made by various governments and organisations have been very successful. A hundred years ago numbers of white rhino had dropped as low as 50–100. Today they have increased to over 11,000. The other four species, however, are critically endangered, the Sumatran and Javan in particular.

The Sumatran rhinos are the most difficult to protect because of the dense foliage in which they live, and because they are scattered throughout different national parks. If their jungles can be protected, the Sumatran tiger and the orang-utan will also benefit.

The sand colour on this map shows the range of the five rhino species in 1800. The five tiny patches of different colours show where the species live today. It gives a rough indication as numbers fluctuate all the time. On 1 February 2006 one lonely black rhino was living in Rwanda. Is it still there?

There are two subspecies of white rhino, five subspecies of black rhino, one species of Indian rhino, two subspecies of Javan and two subspecies of Sumatran.

Rhino's range in 1800

Rhino's range today

White rhino	11,115
Black rhino	3,606
Indian rhino	2,400
Sumatran rhino	300
Javan rhino	67

Approximate numbers recorded in June 2004

NEPAL

INDIA

Arabian Sea

Bay of Bengal

VIETNAM

South China Sea

CENTRAL AFRICAN
REPUBLIC

ETHIOPIA

CAMEROON

KENYA

MALAYSIA

DEMOCRATIC
REPUBLIC
OF CONGO

SUMATRA

BORNEO

Indian Ocean

TANZANIA

JAVA

ZAMBIA

ZIMBABWE

NAMIBIA

BOTSWANA

MOZAMBIQUE

SWAZILAND

SOUTH
AFRICA

2

Thank you

Thank you for buying this book
Thanks to the generosity of the Simon Gibson Charitable Trust, The Iliffe Family Charitable Trust, the Manifold Trust and the Rothschild Foundation (who have supported the production costs), income from these books will go to support the Indian and Sumatran rhinos. I have never seen a Sumatran one. I am told that they have furry ears and that their bodies are covered in bristly orange hair when they are young. That is all I need to know.

If you have bought the book from Save the Rhino International or the Zoological Society of London then 50 per cent of the cover price will go to those organisations. If you have bought it from a bookshop, then the profit will go to Save the Rhino.

Save the Rhino International
This is a UK-registered charity that works to conserve populations of endangered rhinoceros species in the wild. It does this through a number of measures including: community conservation programmes; environmental education programmes; anti-poaching and monitoring patrols; research and veterinary work.
For more information visit their website: *www.savetherhino.org*

Tiger
If you have enjoyed this book, please look out for one on the tiger, also published by Silver Jungle. It can be ordered from *www.21stCenturyTiger.org* or from your local bookshop.

Many friends have helped with advice and encouragement, but there are some who have played a very large role in the production of this book.

Particular thanks to Quentin Newark for his longstanding support and to George Gibson for his continued interest in the project.

Many thanks also to Cathy Dean, Director of Save the Rhino International, who has been consistently enthusiastic and helpful; and Kees Rookmaaker, THE rhinocerologist.

Many thanks to Nicholas Serota, Annabel Ossel, Ian McHale, Dido Sheffield, Jane Morris, Slaney Begley, Paola Faoro, Stephen Coates, Elisabeth Scheder-Bieschin, Tom Hope, Nat Jansz, Matilda Moreton, Annabel Huxley, Libby Wiener, Natasha Seery and John Nicoll.

Finally, many thanks to Patrick and Gabriel for their patience and to my husband, Simon, who keeps pointing out that he supports not only me and the family, but also five species of rhino. A heavy load to bear.

Picture credits

Artothek
p. 39 Jan van Kessel, ©Blauel/Gnamm

Bridgeman Art Library
pp. 13C, 15 Dürer, 33 Longhi,
43 ©Salvador Dalí. Gala-Salvador Dalí Foundation, DACS, London 2006

British Library
p. 23 Kipling (Add. 59840 f.19; Add. 59840 f.20) courtesy of A P Watt Ltd on behalf of The National Trust for Places of Historic Interest or Natural Beauty

Eric Carle
pp. 20, 21 rhino and caterpillar reproduced with permission from Eric Carle. Caterpillar from *The Very Hungry Caterpillar*. Copyright ©1969 and 1987 by Eric Carle. All rights reserved

Christie's Images Ltd
p. 9 ©The Andy Warhol Foundation for the Visual Arts, Inc./ARS, NY, and DACS, London 2006. Courtesy Ronald Feldman Fine Arts, New York.
p. 11 Khmer frieze, p. 17 Jean-G Prêtre

Robert Estall Agency
p. 7 ©David Coulson/Robert Estall Agency

Harappa.com
Courtesy Dept. of Archaeology and Museums, Govt. of Pakistan
pp. 13 A, ©J.M. Kenoyer, 13D, ©Harappa Archaeological Research Project
p. 46 ©R.H. Meadow

Harry N. Abrams
p. 41 first published by Harry N. Abrams, Inc., in 2002. Copyright ©1990 by Laurent de Brunhoff. All rights reserved

Kunsthistorisches Museum, Vienna
p. 27 Katharina

Map
p. 45 drawn by Roger Taylor
©Silver Jungle Ltd

Mobilier National, Paris
p. 29 photo: Philippe Sébert

The Rhino Resource Centre
p. 2 detail of a Roman mosaic, 3rd–4th century AD, Piazza Armerina, Sicily
p. 13 B, p. 19

Nico van Strien, IRF
pp. 4–5 drawings of five rhinos

Philip Wilson Publishers
p. 25 copied with permission from T.H. Clarke, *The Rhinoceros from Dürer to Stubbs, 1515–1799*

The briefest of bibliographies

I have consulted many books and am very grateful to the ZSL, the British Library, the Linnean Society, SOAS and the Natural History Library for the public service they provide. One book in particular should be mentioned: *The Rhinoceros from Dürer to Stubbs, 1515–1799* by T.H. Clarke. THE book, now out of print. The 'mature' reader can find out more about Clara in *Clara's Grand Tour* by Glynis Ridley. For younger readers, there is much to discover on the website of the International Rhino Foundation: *www.rhinos-irf.org*

Published by Silver Jungle Ltd
PO Box 51793, London NW1W 9AZ

©Joanna Skipwith and
Silver Jungle Ltd 2006

ISBN
0-9552652-1-5
978-0-9552652-1-1

FSC
Mixed Sources
Cert no. SGS-COC-0620
© 1996 FSC

Below
Mother and son doing what rhinos love
doing best. These Sumatran ones were
photographed by David Jenike at
Cincinnati Zoo, the only zoo in the past
100 years that has managed to breed a
Sumatran rhino. When the Venetian
explorer Marco Polo visited Sumatra in
1298 he saw several of them and took it
upon himself to break the news to
Europeans that the unicorn was
'altogether different from what we
fancied'. 'They delight much to abide in
mire and mud.' Europe was not ready for
this shocking revelation and decided to
ignore it.

Page 46
Two rhinoceros figurines
Early Indus valley civilisation
2600–1900 BC
Terracotta
Harappa Museum, Pakistan

And finally from Ogden Nash:

Farewell, farewell, you old rhinoceros,
I'll stare at something less prepoceros.